Pisgah Press was established in 2011 to publish and promote works of quality offering original ideas and insight into the human condition, the realm of knowledge, and the world around us.

Copyright © 2021 Pisgah Press

Printed in the United States of America

Released by ArsPoetica
an imprint of Pisgah Press, LLC
PO Box 9663, Asheville, NC 28815
www.pisgahpress.com

Cover design: Bill LaRocque
Book layout: A.D. Reed, MyOwnEditor.com

All rights reserved. No part of this publication may be reproduced, stored in a retrieval system, or transmitted, in any form or by any means, electronic, mechanical, photocopying, recording, or otherwise, without the prior written permission of Pisgah Press, except in the case of quotations in critical articles or reviews.

Library of Congress Cataloging-in-Publication Data
The Barricaded Bards
Osher Lifelong Learning Center
Library of Congress Control Number: 2021902636

ISBN-13: 978-1-942016-62-5
Poetry/Collections

First Edition
First Printing
March 2021

Barricaded Bards:
Poems from the Pandemic

Compiled by Jay Jacoby

Edited by Victoria Bender,
Karen Depew, Ann Tobias
Karson, & Nelson Sartoris

Pisgah Press IP
Asheville, NC

INTRODUCTION

Petrarch, Dante, Shakespeare all wrote during times of quarantine and epidemic.

So, too, have poets at the Osher Lifelong Learning Institute (OLLI) at the University of North Carolina Asheville. When Covid-19 precluded the many face-to-face gatherings that occurred prior to the shutdown, a group of seventeen OLLI poets with a passion to continue writing and sharing their work with fellow writers assembled online. They call themselves the Barricaded Bards.

OLLI Asheville has long had an active, talented poetry community. In addition to dozens of poetry writing courses offered over the years, there are two active Poetry Special Interest Groups that meet monthly. Four years ago, the OLLI Authors reading program was initiated. This quarterly program provides a forum for two OLLI writers to showcase their talents. There are also several other small groups of OLLI poets that meet biweekly.

In mid-March, 2020, these activities came to a sudden halt when Covid-19 caused OLLI to close its doors. With intimate poetic interaction stymied, the sense of community among OLLI poets was threatened. But OLLI poets would not be thwarted. Victoria Bender and Nelson Sartoris reached out to OLLI's poets and the Barricaded Bards was created.

Each week one member of the Bards would select a topic. On the basis of this prompt, poets would write a poem for that week and email it to all the others. Half the fun was the challenge to write on a wide variety of thoughtful, unusual, and amusing topics. The readers would then provide feedback for the poet to consider. The cycle would repeat the following week on a new topic. Many of these poems found their way into a special "Cabin Fever" supplement of the *OLLI Observer*, the weekly newsletter of OLLI Asheville.

Introduction

Although the Barricaded Bards still continue to contribute work during the pandemic shutdown, the poems in this book represent our efforts during only the first thirty-one weeks of poetic exchanges. Each member self-selected four of their poems for inclusion.

The Barricaded Bards hope you enjoy these poems.

Weekly Prompts for the Barricaded Bards

Below is a list of the prompts/topics for the poems appearing in this collection. The name of the Bard who proposed the assignment appears in parentheses:

Week 1 (Victoria Bender): Write a poem about a real event, one which affected people outside your family and friends, although your poem may explore the event on a personal level.

Week 2 (Carol Booth): One of my favorite collections of poetry is Pablo Neruda's *Odes to Common Things*. It includes poems about ordinary items in our homes—a table, chair, an onion, a pair of handmade socks and many more. In this new week of being barricaded, let's do likewise—write about a "common thing."

Week 3 (Karen Depew): Write an ekphrastic poem. Through the imaginative act of narrating and reflecting on the "action" of a painting or sculpture, amplify and expand its meaning. Please include a photo of the artwork along with your poem.

Week 4 (Kim Hayes): This has been a beautiful spring that has been marred, sadly, by COVID-19. For me, it's been hard, even in the strange quietness of my isolation, to appreciate the simple beauty around me. I invite you to join me in setting aside worries, fears and frustrations for just a little while, taking time instead to write about what is beautiful.

Week 5 (Jay Jacoby): Do any of us need to be reminded that we live in a time of cancellations, suspensions, postponements—of putting things on a back burner? We may see this as a blessing or a curse. So, what swims into your poetic mind when you contemplate the word "hiatus"? You need not allude to the current pandemic in response to this challenge, but you are free to do so if you wish.

Weekly Prompts for the Barricaded Bards

Week 6 (Ann Karson): I'm troubled that Climate Change has almost been forgotten, and this is Earth Day week. Although the virus has drawn our attention for good reason, Climate Change is actually the bigger crisis. So, I suggest that we make our focus Climate Change or the looser concept of Climate.

Week 7 (Bonnie Law): Explore your internal landscape, utilizing opposites/opposing forces, and the way the experience(s) of these forces affected, or influenced, perhaps shifted, or changed your perspective in life. If this topic doesn't feel amenable, then write about rugs or floors, or both rugs and floors.

Week 8 (Bill Petz): Write a poem about a teacher or mentor whom you experienced first-hand; what did you learn? how did you learn it? what was the person like? how did you meet? have the lessons lasted? have you paid it forward? any tension? reluctance to learn? Whatever or wherever the idea/subject takes you.

Week 9 (Nelson Sartoris): Write a poem about "Time"—any aspect—personal, objective, theoretical. Take the topic wherever it leads you.

Week 10 (Paul "Schepp" Scheberle): Write a poem about "unexpected kindness."

Week 11 (Sarah Scott): Write a poem about "Risk."

Week 12 (Judy Upjohn): Write about a specific moment (past, present, future) when fear was/is/will be deleted/defeated by beauty.

Week 13 (Wendy Wieber): Write a poem about one of your first memories from infancy or childhood.

Week 14 (Kay Duncan): Compose a poem using this as your launch pad: "All of this good life is surrounded by the ambient feeling that at any given moment, a black person is being killed in the street or in his home by the armed hatred of a fellow American."

Week 15 (Dick Horvath): Write a poem about chance. I've been reflecting lately on the interplay of freedom and chance, order and randomness—luck (good and bad).

Week 16 (Tom Milroy): Write a poem about "Rocks, Sand or Soil."

Week 17 (Jane Elizabeth Wallace): Write a poem about the word "Motion" and take it wherever it leads you.

Week 18 (Victoria Bender): Write about anything you want BUT use a new-to-you word appropriately somewhere in your poem. And underline it or bold it or color it to identify it.

Week 19 (Carol Booth): Light at the end of the tunnel, darkest before the dawn, golden years. As poets we try to avoid clichés. Choose a cliché or proverb or old wives' saying as your title, and see where it leads you.

Week 20 (Karen Depew): Write a poem about what brings you joy; your own Ode to Joy.

Week 21 (Kim Hayes): Dig through those old family albums, choose a photograph (the older and more sepia-toned and faded, the better), and write a poem about it. Note—the photo doesn't have to be a family photo. Dig as deep as you like. Invent a long-lost uncle. Anything counts. No telling what you'll come up with. And if you can, include the photo with your poem.

Week 22 (Jay Jacoby): Write something about the music that you live to. What show tune/s, or doo-wop ballad/s, or aria/s, or torch song/s, or symphony/s, or folk anthem/s is/are woven into the fabric of your soul? What soundtrack gets you through the day?

Week 23 (Ann Karson): I propose Wind of Change as a theme phrase. It can be used as a whole or in separate parts and can be used to consider nature (think climate or just wind in the trees) or politics or anything else.

Week 24 (Bill Petz): Use a favorite one sentence quote by someone most of us would know as the jumping off point for your poem. If possible, let's avoid the current political and health crisis, not because poetry should not go there, it must, but to make a space, even for a moment, out from under the pressing weight on our lives.

Week 25 (Nelson Sartoris): Write a poem about your hometown or neighborhood with an emphasis on how experiences there affected or shaped you (or pick a place where you lived/worked for a good part of your life).

Week 26 (Sarah Scott): Write a poem about curiosity. Let that lead you anywhere your curiosity takes you.

Week 27 (Wendy Wieber): Writing about a journey (internal or external) during this time of little physical travel might be healing. It could take the form of a remembered/desired visit to a place or people, a path, a Jack Kerouac "trip," or whatever "journey" brings up for poets.

Week 28 (Kay Duncan): Write a poem that springs from and includes the words, "What's next?"

Week 29 (Dick Horvath): Assume the persona of a commonly known fictional character (from a novel, cartoon, comic-strip, nursery rhyme) and write a poem speaking in that character's voice.

Week 30 (Tom Milroy): Write a poem about something you don't understand.

Week 31 (Jane Elizabeth Wallace): Chaucer's *Canterbury Tales* gave us the enticing seven deadly sins. This week pick one or more and write away. For those of you who don't keep track of sins, they are pride, greed, lust, envy, gluttony, wrath, and sloth.

Acknowledgements

The Barricaded Bards gratefully acknowledge

Catherine Frank, Executive Director of the Osher Lifelong Learning Institute at the University of North Carolina at Asheville. Catherine encouraged, supported, and helped to promote the Barricaded Bards' project, publishing our work, along with relevant links and illustrations, every week in our newsletter, the *OLLI Observer*.

Bill LaRocque, an extraordinary illustrator and teacher at OLLI, who is responsible for the cover design of this volume.

Dedication

We dedicate this anthology to poets everywhere—
past, present, and future.

Barricaded Bards:

Poems from the Pandemic

Contents

Introduction iv
Weekly Prompts vi

Poems

Victoria Bender
   Chicxulub 2
   October, 1347 3
   Force-Ripened 4
   Wisconsin, Fall 1930 6

Carol Booth
   Red Kite 10
   Sergei and Sir Malcolm 11
   The Few 12
   Gaslighting 14

Karen Depew
   Hiatus 18
   Mugshot 19
   Inheritance 20
   Slothfulness 21

Kay Duncan
   Conjugating on Hiatus 24
   Legacy 26
   Once Upon a Dream 27
   Who Gets To Breathe? 28

Kim Hayes
   Painted Rocks 32
   Beauty's Beasts 33
   Bucket List 34
   Super 36

Richard Horvath
   Pompei A.D. 79 38
   Emmett Till 40
   Misophonia 42
   Joy 43

Jay Jacoby
   On Hiatus 46
   Apikoros: A Confession 48
   Looking for Dad at the CVS 49
   You Do the Math 50

Contents

Ann Tobias Karson
- Spring, 2020 54
- Song [a tanka chain] 55
- Mourning [an inverted-haiku chain] 56
- Question 58

Bill Petz
- Tabula Rasa 60
- Got Him 61
- What's Next? 62
- Home Town Red Hook, NY 64

Nelson Sartoris
- Word Windows 66
- Clothes Make the Man 67
- Primary Things 68
- I Pledge Allegiance 69

Sarah Scott
- Comeuppance 72
- Wind of Ceaseless Change 73
- In Praise of Blake's One-Liner 74
- Question 75

Judy Upjohn
- Hiatus Like a Summer Child 78
- Lessons of the Cornfield 80
- Yes, but the Triangle 81
- Floored Humble 82

Elizabeth Wallace
- Hurricane Moon 86
- Early June Peas 88
- The Unknowing 90
- Firefly Fugue 92

WB Wieber
- Cherries and Chance 94
- The Lonely Wife's Secret 97
- Wild Dogwood 98
- The Song of Everywhen 100

Notes on Contributors 102

Victoria Bender

CHICXULUB

OCTOBER, 1347

FORCE-RIPENED

WISCONSIN, FALL 1930

CHICXULUB
Victoria Bender

First fire, then flood,
then Earth itself
screamed
quaking from every fault,
every plate. Mountains fell,
oceans rose, molten burning
earth filled sky,
wind roared like souls
of murderous beasts.
There was nowhere
to hide.

If they were near enough
to see it, they were dead,
quickly,
there would be no time
for even instinct.
A fast death,
that was best.

For the rest,
there was twilight.
Sky first glowed red
then quickly sank to dark.
Ash fell, acid rain,
toxic air, ozone gone.
Sun could not warm the earth
nor grow the plants,
a place of almost certain death.

And yet,
and yet,
and yet

because of it,

we are here.

Prompt #6

In October 1347, 12 ships entered Messina harbor, bringing the Black Death to Europe. The citizens believed it was proof that Armageddon was at hand with the 4 horsemen of the apocalypse, war, famine, pestilence, and death. Pestilence rode a gray horse and death, a pale horse.

OCTOBER, 1347   Victoria Bender

Twelve ships, newly painted white and
palest gray, enter Messina's harbor
with goods abandoned by lost souls
outside the gates of Hell—
available if one can pay the price.

Twelve ships, priest blessed and backed by
rich men's gold, dock with exotic wares.
Crowds gather first in interest then in fear.
Rumors move and grow like smoke, inhaled
bit by bit 'til lungs cough black phlegm

streaked with blood. Sometimes fear is faster
screaming "Run! Run! It's coming now!" and even
those who don't know why they're running, run.
Twelve ships, and from eleven no one
waved from decks nor called to shore.

But from the twelfth, the captain and first mate,
garbed white and palest gray, smiled at the crowd.
Too late the ships were pushed back to the sea,
ghost ships to ride the waves like stallions
with their riders, pale and gray.

Prompt #1

FORCE-RIPENED
Victoria Bender

She sits in the hard chair in a
room with dirty yellow walls;
a television's s'posed to block
the sound of what's going on
around her, but she knows.
She has old eyes, already tired,
a child made to do a woman's work,
like all the other girls whose mamas
try or half try or don't try at all.

At the edge of fifteen
she's had years of being a mother.
There was a man who laughed her laugh
and taught her how to dance,
who died or left, it doesn't matter which,
he's never coming back.
And that left them and mama.
"You watch 'em" mama says
just before she leaves for work
or loving, or drink or all the other
things that take her from home.
But mama stocks the fridge with food
and sometimes leaves an extra treat
and when she turns to go she says
"You watch 'em."

So she watches; she loves this family.
Loves the sweaty head of little Felix,
sleeping next to eight-year-old Amanda.
That one's trouble; three times now
she's had to go to school explaining
how their mother has to work, can't
be there to meet. Doesn't say
Mama can't be there, period.
Doesn't say she works third shift
isn't there when they get home and
not back when they leave.

They prob'ly know. It's where you work
when you have nothing but somehow
are still alive at 30; 40 would be a miracle
unless, of course, it's disability and that
is bound to happen sometime.
The factory, that's where they all end up
canning fruit from places even worse
than here, where unripe fruit is picked
to reach its final sweetness in the boat
giving the factory a sweet sad
smell with carcasses of used-up fruit
buzzing with the always-present flies.

She thinks about the factory,
the unnatural sweetness
of force-ripened fruit. It isn't right,
the taste, something important missing—
maybe five more days of sunshine, maybe another rain or
nutrients still coming from the roots.
In the end, it will happen as it always does.
Fruit will be picked too early and force ripened
on the boat. But always a piece or two escapes
the picker's hand, and ripens on the tree.

Prompt #18

WISCONSIN, FALL 1930 — Victoria Bender

Pauline, the tough-looking little girl
sitting next to her big brother
has been playing hard.
The hem on one leg of her
too-short pants is ripped out,
and the shirt is streaked with dirt.
Ted's pants are frayed and worn;
he holds a pinwheel. They are sitting
in a wagon next to a well-kept farmhouse,
the walkway swept of leaves.

By next year, the farm
will be foreclosed and they'll
have to move to town.
Their Dad will take a traveling job
selling farm supplies.
They will be lucky though,
they'll have a couple acres
with a garden and some hens.
One day, someone will steal
groceries from their car.

Years later, Pauline will tell
her children how her mother
shook her head, said, "They must
need them more than we do."
and threw some extra water
in the soup.

Prompt #21

Carol Booth

RED KITE

SERGEI AND SIR MALCOLM

THE FEW

GASLIGHTING

RED KITE   Carol Booth

I stand on the brink,
gazing horror-struck, into a pit
of rocks and pinnacles, detritus of a mine.
Bile surges in my throat.
Under my red nylon wrapping,
the hairs on my arms stand up.
Terror grips my belly.
There is no place to flee.

look up

Above me soars the red kite.
See his rufous breast feathers,
wings spread, black and white,
tail opened wide to balance beak.

come

And, leaving fear behind me
on the mountainside, I step out,
my arms stretched wide,
                              I glide,
            I soar.

I am red kite.

Prompt #12

SERGEI AND SIR MALCOLM   Carol Booth

Vibrant violins chase round the meadow,
leaping with energy and life, calling
to the fluttering flute. The oboe
gently paddles, webbed feet
rippling through the cellos.

Clarinet creeps on velvet paws,
slips through waving grass toward
the squabbling winds at water's edge.
Strings shriek to warn, up flies the flute
into the safety of the tree.

The grim bassoon strides out,
reins in the strings, and locks the gate,
gruffly warning of French horns
lurking in the forest, and sure enough
the horns emerge, hungry, looking for a meal.

Oblivious the oboe swims among the reeds,
nibbles on weed, inches closer to the edge.
And with a roar the horns reach out,
swallow her whole, while flute escapes
and whistles sadly from above.

Unfazed the strings soar above the wall,
lasso the growling horns,
holding tight while timpani advance
to take control, and march away,
triumphant.

At the age of eleven, I was taken by my elementary teacher to the new Royal Festival Hall, perched on the bank of the River Thames. The Saturday morning children's concert was conducted by Sir Malcolm Sargent, my first experience of a real concert. It is etched in my memory.

Prompt #22

Never in the field of human history was so much owed by so many to so few. —Sir Winston Churchill, August 1940

THE FEW   Carol Booth

Morning and evening they faced off
across the valley, the giant striding out,
nine feet tall and shining in bronze armor.
"Send out your champion" he roared.
For forty days the king cowered,
seeking someone bigger, braver.
Then the shepherd boy stepped up
with sling and stone and felled the giant.
        The many saved by the one.

The dragon spewed fire and poison
on the land, fouling the fields and wells.
They offered a sheep, then two, a man,
then children drawn by lot, and finally the lot fell
on the daughter of the king. No-one
would give their child to take her place,
but as she faced her doom, the knight rode up
and killed the gruesome fiend.
        The many saved by the one.

The summer sky was checkered
by the Spitfire trails, dogging the enemy
high above the ripening fields.
Each squadron headed out to meet
the waves of fighters from the east.
Young men fell from the sky in burning planes,
while far below the people watched
and prayed for those they lost.
        The many saved by the few.

Times and challenges change.
No longer faced with armored giants,
or fiery dragons, waves of fighter planes,
our battles are insidious.
Sickness, poverty, racism, climate change.
We cannot wait for the one, the few.
    We, the many, must take up the fight.

Prompt #24

GASLIGHTING Carol Booth

Gaslighting is a form of psychological manipulation in which a person or a group covertly sows seeds of doubt in a targeted individual or group, making them question their own memory, perception, or judgment, often evoking in them cognitive dissonance and low self-esteem

The gas lamps flickered.
Was it real, or her imagination?
He laughed at her. You're crazy.
It's all in your mind.
He lied.　　　　　　　　　*Hold on to your reality.*
　　　　　　　　　　　　　Don't believe the lies.

No one else complained.
It must be your perception.
You're too sensitive.
It's fine for all the rest.
He lied.　　　　　　　　　*Hold on to your reality.*
　　　　　　　　　　　　　Don't believe the lies.

That's just the way he speaks.
He's always crude. Take no notice.
Keep your distance.
It doesn't mean a thing.
They lied.　　　　　　　　*Hold on to your reality.*
　　　　　　　　　　　　　Don't believe the lies.

He said he didn't hit her.
She just fell. She's clumsy,
bruises easily, criticizes all the time.
That black eye was all her fault.
He lied.　　　　　　　　　*Hold on to your reality.*
　　　　　　　　　　　　　Don't believe the lies.

We did nothing wrong with Russia,
but what about her emails,
this virus is a sniffle,
to be gone when summer comes.
He lied. *Hold on to your reality.*
Don't believe the lies.

Prompt #18

Karen Depew

HIATUS

MUGSHOT

INHERITANCE

SLOTHFULNESS

HIATUS   Karen Depew

Normal routines interrupted,
daily rhythms slowed,
survival demanding adaptation.

Outside my window
a teacher waits,
rooted.
Awakening from winter,
leafless. Dressed only
in drab brown. Silent
in the wind.
Energy directed
downward
into roots
into quiet
into growth.

Prompt #5

MUGSHOT

Karen Depew

Day and night I sit on a shelf, stone-faced,
along with others of my kind.
Harsh fluorescent light wakes me
and the sounds begin.
Grinding, splashing, dripping.

A hand lifts me down.
My bottom makes a clink
on a cold, hard surface.
Burbling starts.
Hot liquid warms my round interior.
An aromatic steam rises from my mouth.

I am picked up, tilted, liquid slides
over my curved lip and passes down
another set of warm, pink lips.
A pause. Contentment.

Prompt #2

INHERITANCE   Karen Depew

Among sepia daguerreotypes
of unsmiling ancestors—
hoop-skirted, hair tightly pulled into buns,
arranged around seated matriarchs or patriarchs—
is a photo of a young woman.
Flowing hair frames a tilted oval face,
soft smile, large eyes stare directly
into the camera.
A rose languidly hangs over her left ear.
No high-necked blouse
only a soft silky shawl
draped to reveal a milky chest.
Did I inherit her boldness?

Prompt #21

SLOTHFULNESS   Karen Depew

wake when sunlight
interrupts dreams
no haranguing alarm
last night's scents linger
on warm sheets
nowhere to go
no one to see
no desire to arise
surrender to indolence

Prompt # 31

BARRICADED BARDS: POEMS FROM THE PANDEMIC

Kay Duncan

CONJUGATING ON HIATUS

LEGACY

ONCE UPON A DREAM

WHO GETS TO BREATHE?   23

CONJUGATING ON HIATUS   Kay Duncan

I am on hiatus
nestled nonchalantly upon it
like the raven perched
above Poe's chamber door
or little Miss Muffet atop her tuffet
no curds and whey for me, thank you,
make mine Haagen-Dazs
Midnight Cookies and Cream

we are on hiatus
ensconced gracefully upon it
divinely unearned and unjustified
a privileged part of the world
lingering in sanitized intermission
anxious for theatre doors to reopen
biding time 'til we return to our seats
and resume the play

they are on hiatus —
NOT —
face to unmasked face
demanded, not asked
essential, yet ill-equipped,
long hours grappling
with an unseen plague
performing on the high wire
without a safety net
disinfecting, stocking, checking, nursing, cooking,
harvesting, cleaning, packaging, delivering, policing
unfortunately, unforgivable, [so sorry],
no bullet-proof vests available

earth is on hiatus
a brief respite of cleaner air
fewer carbon emissions
she can breathe more deeply
see the Himalayas again
the push to launch the economy looms
fossil fuels will flow
the EPA will roll over
corporations will bulldoze
evermore

Prompt #5

LEGACY
Kay Duncan

for Michael Connelly

LA, 1992. Riots roil
and seethe six nights,
finally die down.
A policeman, safe now,
needs a smoke. He heads
into Fortune Liquor.

The counterman waves
his arm, half turning.
Looters took every
last pack in the place.
No cigarettes.
Plenty matches.

The counterman reaches
into his shirt pocket, pulls
out his own smoke,
his only one,
and gives
it to the policeman.

Decades later,
the policeman still
carries that book
of Fortune Liquor matches
in his shirt pocket,
one match gone.

Prompt #10

ONCE UPON A DREAM   Kay Duncan

In another life I was a fairy godmother
kitted out with a magic wand
to wield bibbidi bobbidi boo
over life's necessities, such as
a dress for the prince's ball.

I merely followed the day's
playbook. Never heard a different
drummer, never considered
a road less traveled. I never looked
beyond one dancing date.

Why didn't I winkle her out of
her stepmother's clutches
and into a slot at veterinary school?
Do a long-term fix based on her work ethic
and her aptitude with animals?

I squandered her
to enchanting fickle royalty
by midnight.

WHO GETS TO BREATHE?   Kay Duncan

    oh God, oh God
        oh no, not again
oh yeah . . . yeah
    my precious baby
        another killing
nothing but a lowlife
    they murdered him
        another black man killed
just a thug
    I've lost my reason for living
        yet another murder by a white cop
just a gangbanger
    all our lives we've been living with slain black bodies
        so many, so often, so constant — I had no idea
they're all violent criminals
    he was murdered because he was black
        he was murdered because he was black
he doesn't matter
    they hate us
        a lynching every four days during Jim Crow
I hate these people
    they want us all dead
        a killing by a white cop every two to three days now
I'm law enforcement
    it's open season on us
        why do they keep killing them?
law and order matter
    THIS is my city
        this is my CITY
this is MY city
    I can scarcely breathe
        I need to take slow, deep breaths
I breathe fine

I can't breathe
I can't breathe
I can't breathe
I can't breathe
I can't breathe
I can't breathe
I can't breathe
I can't brea

Prompt #14

Kim Hayes

PAINTED ROCKS

BEAUTY'S BEASTS

BUCKET LIST

SUPER

PAINTED ROCKS   Kim Hayes

She secretly delivers painted rocks,
like benedictions. We find them at dawn,
nestled in our mailbox gardens.

   "Hope"
   for a time
   when we will all
   come out from
   behind closed doors.

   "Be Brave"
   when the fear of sickness
   overrides sickness itself;
   when cureless, we suffer,
   uncared for.

   "Take Time to Play"
   because your laughter
   is a contagion of good,
   from depths of soul
   where healing waits.

   "Joy"
   is stronger than
   fear or sorrow or pain,
   is greater than
   our anger.

   "Peace"
   is a balm in the dark
   when you lay restless,
   losing your faith.
   It comes softly.

Anonymous blessings:
her gift of painted rocks.

                                                      Prompt #10

BEAUTY'S BEASTS   Kim Hayes

No magic kiss rouses her
from her deep coma.
She just finally opens her eyes.
And although she understands
that a happy ending has never
been guaranteed—
> that dragons will always need to be slain;
> that trolls will live under the bridge;
> that the prince is nothing but a toad after all—

she chooses possibility.

Standing there at the edge of
the dark, haunted forest, awake at last,
she chooses to draw a deep breath

and step in.

Prompt #12

BUCKET LIST
Kim Hayes

I will drive to Key West
in a fast, red convertible,
top down, souvenir stops to shop
at every roadside
mom and pop.
Sipping syrupy brown rum things,
I will sit in many bars,
considering Hemingway
and watching all the seven-toed cats
as I pass the day.

And I will find an American desert,
stand panting on the blistered sand
in the spidering, thin shade of
a Joshua tree;
will wait for winter rains
and carpets of cactus flowers;
or will go out in black night,
searching a velvet sky-sea
for the star that made me
from its dust.

And I will go to the Outer Banks
in search of the wild mustangs,
watch them race over dunes
and down to the shore,
pushing, nipping, bickering;
they will roll in the sand,
ragged stallion's harem,
grazing on sea oats and thin grass,
or waiting as storms pass, turned tail
to a stinging wind.

Or I will just carry my coffee to the porch
on a chilly morning, where hummingbirds
sip from one last feeder,
restless, irritable, summoned;
if I feed them again, they will stay
and freeze on the first icy day.
I send them away,
to what they may have missed
on their own distant bucket lists,
imprinted in their DNA.

Prompt #27

SUPER — Kim Hayes

As if it mattered,
I look at the scattered
buttons on the dirty floor,
rumpled tie, pants and shoes
inside the phone booth door,
where I lean unseen,
about to transform
from this uniform
back into day clothes
as if no one knows
how this goes:
humankind, always at stake,
saved on another coffee break,
then, like a speeding bullet,
back in time to pull it
off the press, making deadline
with another headline
that is, but isn't, mine,
as if people can't see
that it's really just me,
that superpowers
are no help for the hours
spent alone in the dark
just being
Clark.

Prompt #29

Richard Horvath

POMPEI A.D. 79

EMMETT TILL

MISOPHONIA

JOY

POMPEI A.D. 79 — Richard Horvath

They wake to the sun
rising over Mt. Vesuvius.
The morning begins to fill with the sounds
of flour grinding in the kitchens
and the bustle of men and women
in the marketplaces
where the stalls hold fresh October fruit
and children play by the fountains
and over there a dog, its rear leg lifted,
pees on the far wall of a villa where
a young boy scrawls crude graffiti.
By noontime the taverns are filling
and the baths are filling
with the waters flowing
from Agrippa's aqueduct in the mountains.
A low rumbling is heard in the distance.

They will not see the setting
of this day's late November sun.
Entombed in ash
their bodies left a void
to be filled with plaster
allowing us to view
their final gestures frozen forever.
A leg raised bent at the knee
in an attitude of escape
a child with outstretched arms
calling for its mother
a mouth forming a sound
we can only guess at
a couple embracing
the startled eyes of an old man.

What draws us here to this museum
to lean in close to view their agony
the suddenness of their death?
Do we see in them something of ourselves?
Do we grieve for them,
these strangers far removed in time?
Or do we grieve for ourselves and those we love
knowing that we too can be
randomly struck down?
We are not immune.
All we can do is look
into the eyes of our loved ones.
All else is incomprehensible.

EMMETT TILL   Richard Horvath

In the early morning hours of
August 28, 1955
a 14-year-old boy is murdered in Mississippi.

In the early morning hours of
August 28, 1955
a 14-year-old-boy is asleep in Connecticut.

In the wee midnight hour
two armed men take the Mississippi boy
from his uncle's house
march him outside
tie him up
and drive him away in a green pick-up truck

In the early morning hours
the Connecticut boy
wakes at dawn
steps outside
breathes fresh air
and feels safe.
That afternoon he was bouncing
in the back of a pick-up truck
on the way to berry picking.

They take him to a barn
the black boy from Chicago
visiting his uncle
in Money Mississippi
they beat and mutilate him.
Someone said he whistled
at a white woman in a candy store.

I have a yellow carnival bird
made of cork and cloth
attached by string to a stick
and when I whirl it
round and round
it whistles.

The uncle in Money Mississippi
waits for the boy's return
but he doesn't come back.
They found his body three days later
in the Tallahatchie River
bound, beaten, shot in the head
dumped from the Black Bayou Bridge.

On that day in August 28, 1955
and the next day and the next
no one told the Connecticut boy
about the boy in Money Mississippi.

No one told him
how terror could be unleashed
unexpectedly
in the dark hours before dawn.

No one told me that a boy my very age
was murdered in Mississippi.

No one told me about Emmett Till.

Prompt #14

MISOPHONIA   Richard Horvath

It's not the fear or loathing
of fermented soybeans
mixed with salt, fungus, and seaweed
but rather, it's the nauseating emotion
that wells up, as from a cesspool,
upon hearing repetitive noises
that can become unbearable—
those bête noirs of irritating sounds
that many suffer from:
the scratching of fingernails across the chalkboard.
the never-ending clacking of computer keys.
the interminable blather at cocktail parties
that drive you into a corner to get quietly drunk.
the dripping faucet at 3 AM.
the smacking of lips after a gulp of beer or a sip of latte.
the almost lewd sounds made by the open-mouth chewer
   of food, the slurping, the crunching.
the 5 AM beeping of the garbage truck backing up outside
   your window.
the cracking of knuckles and clipping of nails in the
   dentist's waiting room.
the grinding and gnashing of teeth.
and for the hapless city-dweller in the country for the
   weekend
the cacophony of noise from creatures of the night.

But here's the rub:
What I wouldn't give to hear again
that most distasteful sound
the incessant clicking of your ballpoint pen.
Two weeks now you're gone.

Prompt #18

JOY
Richard Horvath

It's not the bursting belly
of the piñata
spilling candy
across the lawn

it's deeper more abiding
the nurturing of seeds
In a garden over time

it's the laughter
of children nestled in your arms at night
while you read them stories
before they close their eyes.

it's a dream of honey
dripping from the eaves
of all the houses where you have lived

it's remembering blue shadows
of a winter twilight
a warm kiss with snow
settling softly on eyelids

it's that tender hour at daybreak
when first the sun appears
to shine a light
across a loved-one's sleeping face

it's how the body still sings
in the midst of travail and sorrow.

Prompt #20

Jay Jacoby

ON HIATUS

APIKOROS: A CONFESSION

LOOKING FOR DAD AT THE CVS

YOU DO THE MATH   45

ON HIATUS   Jay Jacoby

*Like failure, chaos contains information that can lead to knowledge—
even wisdom. Like art.*
—Toni Morrison

    HIATUS [hahy-ey-tuhs/haɪˈeɪ təs] noun
1. a space where   2. A time when
   something   nothing
   no longer is   happens.

       abyss,   bre/
       ach,
                c
                h
                a
                s
                m,

    discontinuity,

      emptiness,
                    fis sure,
         gap,
  hollow,   interval,

jaw, knot-
  hole,   leaving

out,   moratorium,
opening,

pause,
              recess, sch

ism,   tunnel,
vacancy,
  womb,   yawn,

              zoning out.

Proto-Indo-European root *ghieh*- "to yawn, gape, be wide open
Originally, the word referred to a gap or opening in something,
such as a cave opening in a cliff.

So why all the negativity?
The pissing and moaning?
The gloom and doom?

GIVE ME A BREAK!

The mouth of the cave, the blackened void, the gaping unknown
is not a terrible darkness but a welcome alternative to certainty:

It is there that we find
"a spacious uncertainty
in which there is
room to act"*

Hiatus = Opportunity/Mindfulness
A chance to discover that another world can be possible.

There is never a space where something no longer is.
There is never a time when nothing happens.

And who among us didn't cherish recess?

*Rebecca Solnit, *Hope in the Dark*

Prompt #5

APIKOROS: A CONFESSION   Jay Jacoby

> "... *these are the ones who have no portion in the world to come:*
> *... an apikoros* [heretic]"
>   —Mishnah Sanhedrin 10:1

"What are you willing to die for?" you ask.

Heart answers, "Family, Friends, and Loved Ones."
Soul answers, "Sunrises and Sunsets, Waterfalls and
    Rivulets."
Mind answers, "Justice, Racial Harmony, Peace on Earth."
Body answers, "Fried Artichokes from *La Reginella*,
Crown Roast of Lamb from Gibby's,
Saltimbocca alla Romana from Victor Café,
Wood-grilled Char with Chanterelles from NOLA,
Seven Boy Curry from Orchard Inn,
Roast Duck from Sun Wah BBQ,
Lobster Quenelles from *La Maisonette*
Tongue and Chopped Liver from Kaufman's,
Veal *Française* and *tagliatelle* from Riccio's,
Filet Mignon and Creamed Spinach from Blue Bell Inn,
Ginger and Scallion Lobster from Red Ginger,
Cheesesteak from Pat's, Jim's, or Dallesandro's."

Appetite wins. Every time.
For the sake of these dozen pleasures,
I would lay down my life.
Not only would I die for them,
but also forfeit my portion
in the world to come.

Prompt #11

LOOKING FOR DAD AT THE CVS   Jay Jacoby

What I remember best are your hands,
not how they once looked, but

how, with Uncle Harry, they swung me above the waves at Atlantic City,
how they raised me to see my face beside yours in the mirror over the sofa,
how they lifted me up to peer into the top drawer of the mahogany dresser.

There was magic in that drawer: cuff-links, hair-brushes, boxes of *Sen-Sen*—
Tiny hard flakes of licorice to banish cigarettes and bourbon from your breath.
You would shake their matchbox containers, dancing to the rhythm of maracas.

But it is your hands, holding me under my arms, that I remember best, and
how, decades later, I would lift my own son up to touch the ceiling light,
how my hands felt under his arms while I sang "Dancing Cheek to Cheek."

At the drug store, among sixteen flavors of *Tic-Tacs*, I discover that *Sen-Sen*
is long ago gone, and I don't have your hands to swing me, raise me, lift me up.
So, I must settle, in aisle five, for your caress in bottles of *Vitalis* and *Old Spice*.

Prompt #13

YOU DO THE MATH   Jay Jacoby

Let the nightmare begin

Calculus: the branch of mathematics that deals with the finding and properties of derivatives and integrals of functions, using methods based on the summation of infinitesimal differences.

1. Evaluate the following integrals:

   a) $\int_0^1 \frac{x^3 - 4x - 10}{x^2 - x - 6} dx$

   b) $\int \arctan\left(\frac{1}{x}\right) dx$

   c) $\int_0^{\frac{\pi}{4}} \sec^3 \theta \tan \theta \, d\theta$

I do not understand any of the words
following "the branch of mathematics."
I do not want to understand them.
Ever.

The University of Cincinnati in 1964.
241 Swift Hall was the Mouth of Hell.
Endlessly, Professor Thorne talks of limits.
Spinning on my y-axis, I beg him to fail me.
He sees hope where clearly there is none.

A gaggle of gearheads surround me in the dorm,
future engineers from Ashtabula to Zanesville,
packing heat—slide rules holstered on their hips.
They drool functions. Integrals run down their chins.

My differences from them are more than infinitesimal.

The walls of my room are plastered
with years' worth of Playboy centerfolds.
The walls of their rooms are neatly hung
with blackboards bearing primitive functions,
Fourier series, and inverse Laplace transforms.

They have come to tutor me into their world,
to save me. I do not want to be saved by anyone
but Donne, Lawrence, cummings, and Thomas's
"The force that through the green fuse drives the flower."

Ann Tobias Karson

SPRING, 2020

SONG [a tanka chain]

MOURNING [an inverted-haiku chain]

QUESTION

SPRING, 2020   Ann Tobias Karson

Today amid our empty streets,
our sense of hidden enemy,
the season, spring, returns and greets
our ongoing year, implacably.

We hide inside or walk alone
yet each her lot with others shares,
as, unperturbed, nature moves on:
beauty consoles as if it cares.

The pretty blossoms say it's spring:
bright hyacinths and daffodils
compel our gaze; our spirits sing
in company with songbirds' trills.

What power has the virus, then,
to spoil our lives? No, we've the option
to focus on this moment's pain
or smile at springtime's invitation.

Prompt # 1

SONG [a tanka chain]   Ann Tobias Karson

At age eleven,
steam train confined for three days,
I heard them singing—
songs inevitable when
young Germans get together.

They weren't sociable:
post-war, they kept to themselves.
Yet concertina
and voice was all they needed
to convey beautiful sound,

enchant a young girl
so recently enemy,
teaching me to seek
beauty in songs and poems
wherever they might be found.

Sounds of steam, of wheels'
rhythmic clattering on rails,
even whistle's voice
unable to drown them out,
gave background to their music.

Using my own words,
inspired, I sang my own song
into train-made wind,
deep mysterious dark of night,
beyond the out-spilling light.

Under starry sky,
head leaning out the window,
for me sounds would meld—
the Germans, the train and me—
into a romantic blend.

Prompt #22

MOURNING [an inverted-haiku chain]   Ann Tobias Karson

Protests convulse the country.
I should be there too.
Age and virus keep me home.
    . . . . .

Apartheid South Africa
put my life at risk.
Somehow protest turned me black.

My life had ceased to matter:
my actions the cause.
But for black folks, true from birth.

And privilege pursued me:
I left for exile
legally, but they could not.
    . . . . .

Here too they're born to blackness.
Born to dark of night.
Does black mean invisible?

If true, they would not be killed.
They are visible
and they are a threat to some.

Here, white, we fear our own guilt,
know we should atone.
For some that's unacceptable.
    . . . . .

It's said black life *is* mourning
lack of normal life,
freedom from anxiety.

Pain, death is not unlikely.
If you're young and black,
hate and fear are in the air.

So true in South Africa
under apartheid.
Even now that's likely true.
. . . . .

True in America too.
Yet can things change here?
Today we see signs of hope.

How can I make my voice count?
I want to shout out.
Must one be young to take part?

I was among the young once.
Now I mourn my youth.
Can my aging voice be heard?
. . . . .

Protests convulse the country.
I should be there too.
Age and virus keep me home.

QUESTION
Ann Tobias Karson

What's next? the rose asks,
the last of summer "left blooming alone,"
her companions "faded and gone."
Is that to be her fate?

When with cold and frost
her petals fall, will that be the end?
Or does she have some meaningful connection
with her source, her parent, the plant
that will survive the winter?

When "new" blooms surface, will they
hold the essence of her? Or will
that essence have dissipated into air
or into the soil where her petals went?
Will there be a sense in which
she'll even know?

What's next for her? Empty dying?
Or some unforeseen resurrection
in which her soul contributes
to an ethereal future
where life of some kind
continues to exist?

What's next?

Prompt #28

Bill Petz

TABULA RASA

GOT HIM

WHAT'S NEXT?

HOME TOWN RED HOOK, NY

TABULA RASA   Bill Petz

No memories of the infant
or young child that was me.
It's pictures of me I remember.
Each a rigid image of a moment
evoking a landscape of what
might have been my life.

Stuffed in winter clothes hugging my brother
both of us smiling real smiles.

At edge of a lake, head cocked,
holding a string of fish, next to my brother.

My mother holding her Bible, flanked
by her sons uncomfortable in church clothes.

Standing straight and tall wearing
cowboy hat and cowboy boots.

Sprawled in a canvas chair
in the midst of family campsite.

Signposts on a young road
overgrown with bramble of time.

Prompt #13

GOT HIM   Bill Petz
in memory of Rayshard Brooks

The hungry prey comes to the salt lick
for essential nutrients. Threatened by the hunters
it turns and runs. The hunter, his license pinned
to his blue jacket, fires twice. Standing over the fallen,
"Got him," he crows.

For generations
the license
has been renewed
by our silence.

Prompt #14

WHAT'S NEXT?   Bill Petz

The carnival is starting to load the trucks after a four-year
    run.
Their GPS set for next stop. The road show hoped
for a longer stay, but people have grown weary of same
old acts. Though actors changed, still same show.

Clown car emptied on cue, red noses and face paint
    disguise
criminal past, they're at home with the carnival. Actors on
    illusory
big stage. In private dark of fitful sleep they know they are
only expendable bit players in a power scheme for more.

Freak show once intriguing curiosities, now uncaged scary
    monsters.
Talking two headed cow no more than a single minded bull
    looking
to hump the bearded lady, 200-year-old storyteller just a
    chain smoker
addicted to tanning beds. The immobile fat man requires a
    forklift, or two.

Unseemly "girlie show" promised to power brokers in
    exchange
for a business license short lived. Contract termination
    buy-outs
completed. Arcade games cheat players who continue to
    play
hoping to beat the system. They couldn't.

"Thrill rides" shorter lines, shorter ride times than Disney,
no height requirements. The carnival would ~~take~~ give
    anybody
~~for~~ a ride. Old, unstable rides. Safety inspectors busy
    elsewhere
or new on the job.

What's next? A kinder, gentler carnival? A less freaky freak show?
Safer rides? Or a circus next time? Big shows, competent actors,
longer rides on the roller coaster? Or no shows, gritty or glitzy, at all?
No scripted misdirection set pieces? Let's load the trucks.

Prompt # 28

HOMETOWN RED HOOK, NY   Bill Petz

After the duel Burr came here to hide
when he learned that Hamilton had died.
We spent our youth hiding here as well
secret thoughts and deeds we'd never tell.

Our gender roles clearly defined
any variations fervently denied.
Sports a show of masculinity
to cover for our shy virginity.

Our lust was barely concealed
until the pregnancies were revealed.
The surprise kids we then raised
made up for lives never praised.

We hid the cigarettes we smoked
long before weed was ever toked.
Petty thefts from the corner store
we knew our parents would deplore.

Fears of uncertain future encroached
as our graduation days approached.
"We Gotta Get Outa This Place" a theme
we could have taken as our meme.

No longer thoughts of happy returns
passion for home no longer burns.

Details of the hidden not exposed
what you need to know now disclosed.

Prompt #25

Nelson Sartoris

WORD WINDOWS

CLOTHES MAKE THE MAN

PRIMARY THINGS

I PLEDGE ALLEGIANCE 65

WORD WINDOWS — Nelson Sartoris

I know you only through your poems,
word windows into your passions, your past,
your frustrations, your dreams.

What further revelations of your soul
will future poems lay bare, what other
illuminating fires burn within?

What furtive cravings smolder deep inside,
things you would never reveal
even through clever metaphoric disguise?

I long to know more, not only the what,
why, and where of you, but the who—
your written words alone do not satisfy.

Or are your poetic allures merely sketches
of an invented personality, a mythical opus
exposing only the skills of a gifted wordsmith?

Is the only way to genuinely know you
to hear your words whispered
with heads on pillows in soft morning light?

Prompt #26

CLOTHES MAKE THE MAN

Nelson Sartoris

He dresses in blue before
morning coffee with his wife.
Badge, service belt, gun
commence his transformation.
He slowly becomes his uniform.

Riot gear, baton, shield, tear gas,
pepper spray, rubber bullets
complete the metamorphosis.
Authority now his persona,
hostility his demeanor.

Ready for battle
against the unarmed enemy,
outfitted like a hammer
protestors become nails,
peace officer disturbing the peace.

Or—perhaps anger, prejudice,
bullying and aggression
were already in his character
before he armored himself in blue
to legally assert his littleness.

Prompt #14

PRIMARY THINGS

Nelson Sartoris

along the path midst fallen
rustling rusty leaves
a flash of yellow,
a primary feather in primary color,
its intricate Velcro-like barbules
locked together for lift.

yellow-shafted flicker plume
left for me as gift for you,
a trace of former hurried flights
now fixed nicely in your hat.

further up the trail another find,
this one primary blue
with laced dark bands,
joy for you from a blue jay,

then, as if by fate,
a cardinal's primary
burns radiantly for you
in sunlight on the forest floor,

your cap now adorned with
primary makings of a rainbow
from avian discards.

share with me
the feathers you find,
together we'll take wing.

Prompt #4

Flags are bits of colored cloth that governments use first to shrink-wrap people's brains and then as ceremonial shrouds to bury the dead.   —Arundhati Roy

I PLEDGE ALLEGIANCE   Nelson Sartoris

*
*
*   colored cloths divide us into tribes,
*
*   enflame feral fabric of naive minds,
*
*   cloak humanity of alleged enemies,
*
*   mask horrors of soldiers slaughtered
*
* then become burial shrouds to honor young warriors
*
* seduced by virile threads of patriotic myths woven
*
* into vivid nationalistic banners once so proudly hailed;
*
* yet with civilization in grave jeopardy flags still wave.
*
*
*
*
*
*
*
*
*
*
*
*
*
*
*`

Prompt #24

Sarah Scott

COMEUPPANCE

WIND OF CEASELESS CHANGE

IN PRAISE OF BLAKE'S ONE-LINER

QUESTION 71

COMEUPPANCE   Sarah Scott

Gaia has a way to heal:
sicken the deadliest predator
with a brilliant intruder
that enters unseen, thrives,
spreads with stealth.
Our might, our guns and bombs, are no defense.

Mere toddlers as a species,
we rampage if unchecked.
What we want, we take as ours.
Other species get no claim,
extinctions go uncounted.
Not one threatened our survival.

We are in need of learning we are earth—
at best, life's way to know and love itself.

We are under occupation now,
humbled by this invader whose reign
falls on the just and the unjust.
Meanwhile, skies blue, water clears,
and we are given time,
we are given time to learn.

Prompt #6

WIND OF CEASELESS CHANGE   Sarah Scott

The suddenness of it
the menacing stealth
thrust us
into strange new ways.
The shoving just won't stop.

A squirrel runs along a maple branch.
A breeze, soft and familiar, flicks new-green leaves.

The door to worked-for dreams
slammed shut
by the force
of what abruptly is.
Our door to all that is uncertain
blown wide open.
Distanced
against our nature
most cruelly in lonely deaths.

A squirrel gathers to store.
A breeze, signaling, rustles crisp leaves.

Who we were
who we thought we would always be
altered now
by this ill wind
anybody's guess how long.
Soon? Ever?
What then?
What will life
for each of us billions,
what will life as we lost it
have become?

Prompt #23

You never know what is enough unless you know what is more than enough.

　　　　　　　—William Blake, *The Marriage of Heaven and Hell*

IN PRAISE OF BLAKE'S ONE-LINER　　　　　　Sarah Scott

When I found it
I was home from college.
The line went back with me in September
written on a sheet of paper
taped to my dorm wall.
Not the dictum my genteel mother would have chosen
but one that would've heard my father's knowing laugh.
Blake's canny wisdom gave me what I most sought
permission
absolution.

Still does.
So I give it to you
the next time your shoulds
throw shame;
the next time you chide
yourself and your inherently
limited batch of facts
for not knowing the future;
the next time you're not perfect.

Prompt #24

QUESTION   Sarah Scott

Question for you:
Can you ask Google a question that hasn't been posed?
One that doesn't in an instant
suggest ways to finish your question
based on all those before yours?
Can you submit to Google an original question?
Not something absurd,
not *What will happen after orangutans learn to walk on water?*
although that would surely bring up options
and that chiding *Did you mean?*

What's next, Google?
I just asked it that.
Up popped eighteen pages of links before I could blink twice.

Prompt #28

Judy Upjohn

HIATUS LIKE A SUMMER CHILD

LESSONS OF THE CORNFIELD

YES, BUT THE TRIANGLES

FLOORED HUMBLE

HIATUS LIKE A SUMMER CHILD   Judy Upjohn

Hugh hate us
High ate us
Hyatt us
Hi. At us

No gap, only gape. A filled word foiling its —
not a fissure, cleft or pause,
invitation to memory flood...

Like summer camp or campless summers even better spent
in sandbox castle building all innocence of world & knowledge
when childhood ending day launched:

"The Easter bunny is not real, nor toothfairy nor sandman"
hateful Hugh pronounced, stomped & toothed at my chagrin

        Momentary hiatus fill: NOOOOO

Disappointment like stuffing fell out of the me I knew onto
    sand
but barely enough of a gap for a Hi let alone Hiatus, & so...
8 x 8 foot square's surrounding desert fill of realworld
    dunes
dragged me from ex-childhood misery
into the Have to: princess needs were real & dire, & I,
architect of her escape from prison tower
tore more cardboard from Dad's 8 x 8 inch
laundered shirts to level the landing ramp.
Every princess needs an airport

But
a snag
        Knowledge lacuna: ARGHHH
          "High ate us!"

Princess calling out from high, in desperate need (of hiatic
    escape!) so royal *We*
hauled out Websters & Britannica: how how how *do* planes
    take off & land?
Runway ramp rising up? Sloping down? Think think

Think of sailing those folded planes
from the Hyatt's high floor
too high to see how they crashed or landed—
up to launch, down to land? How to stop? Must be th'other
    way 'round, but no—

                HIATUS!

Meanwhile, the princess languished, tomatoes reddened,
    birdlings gaped
their mouths for mamafood, &

the architect wore hair of sand
& no fairytales but the awe
of question-filled worlds
all of a summer's hiatus

LESSONS OF THE CORNFIELD Judy Upjohn

Bobbing along on striped shirt shoulders
high atop through cornfield rows
He pointed astonished views wayout
over fields, fences, neighbors' valleys
long views of wide futures
adulthood's borders
worlds miles-foreign from tiny habitation
under my mother's dressing table
or the crib where I still in my room
of knotty pineholes
& Kelly's Weary Willie & other Kelly's Pogo
in the room that would burn its walls to husky bark
& spread inhabitants to temporary habitations
over fields, fences, neighbors' valleys
past childhood—

Uncle's house bordering cornfield's late husks
I too large for shoulders, small enough
for his fingers wayward along adult borders
burning young trust
over fields, fences, neighbors' valleys
past comprehension—

Visceralized bobbling through cornfields's sharp
    shoulders—
sensorial confusion, cornfield & intrusion

Yet pleasure remains in imperfect division
astonished by fields, fences, neighbors' valleys

    Look the lesson
    Look the long view—
    astonishment still

Prompt #13

YES, BUT THE TRIANGLES   Judy Upjohn

Last night
        I dreamed again
of the fire   (he said
ponderously)   Tentatively I replied with   Yes! The
    triangles!

He paused   Trauma (said
accusingly)   Not for me, I replied
                WHAT? (he loudly
countered)   How so? You think of it often   I do, I said
     You remember the night   I do
     You remember the flames, the smoke, the window
         pane   I do, it broke
             ONLY (he countered)
when smashed by the hurled TV set

I paused   the roof (I recalled)
       glass underfoot (I recalled)
          in my hair, blood somewhere
& the fear that we'd all
       FALL INTO THE FIREY ROOM BELOW
    (drama in the local news,
my desk moves to the drinking fountain at school,
     coughing up lessons)

Easy recall, I can live it anew, hot cut soles, screaming sister,
     waiting to drop through the
     roof
          (but then)   through the night
    catapulted orange shapes,
triangles spinning head over tail through green darkness
      windows exploding
WINDOWS EXPLODING he shouted
              Yes. I recall. No fear at
all. Only color & beauty,
     for some moments, at least
           Only awe.

Prompt #12

FLOORED HUMBLE   Judy Upjohn

Stand tall!
Stand proud!
Stand certain of
that gendered-sexist-racist-classist-ageist-
call-it-what-you-will
               (what we will & you won't)
                    BIGOTED
stance, your master of my private universe
of smugness stance—
They say take the high road
I say go down, go sting your nostrils
on the below-yourself beliefs
you walk on, stomp on, skip on
ignoramously with impunity
I speak of myself when I say
Face your floorboards
Lay your locked mind down
Fall if that's what it takes
face first
Let the real-out-there slap the small opinion out of you

Out of me the day
I thought to know
cream rises to the top, no matter
ravages of poverty's multi-squid-armed
breaking young backs

        2 buses, 2 subways, 2 hours
           to school's prison security (one door, 4 cops,
locked cafeteria, locked
        bathrooms, armed escorts to and fro all inner doors
locked—no key
           out of luck)
        2 buses, 2 subways, 2 hours back
        each days' strategic loopwork
        a self-ostracizing wayaround necessity

                        from crimework & brownblackwhite
firestorm & copdeath
                        & gangs who consider him legacy

                        Abandon the easy, the mainstream
                        the takenforgranted
                        & find church a refuge longday after & after
                        for homework, for safety, for mother's belief
in belief
                        his belief a far third concern behind

The boy tagged by teachers
"leadership potential" will make it out—
right?
Will make it out easy as cream rises
to richness, to skim
for society's goodness—
so many in need, why spend on him?
His fifteen years surely greenshoot his longevity
elasticity, children's resilience he surely has
even with 2.5 years
                        4 buses, 4 subways, 4 hours a schoolday—
                        thank god for schooldays
                        a self-ostracizing wayaround necessity
                        from crimework & brownblackwhite
firestorm & copdeath
                        & gangs who consider him legacy—

Surely, he'll make it out!

Is it needful to say my facedown day
imposed by real-out-there smackdown
slapped open the smoothskull containment
I thought was right
my right as a standup woman
& forever challenged my ignorant
rightminded sympathy

                                                    Prompt #14

Elizabeth Wallace

HURRICANE MOON

EARLY JUNE PEAS

THE UNKNOWING

FIREFLY FUGUE

HURRICANE MOON   Elizabeth Wallace

the village is small, hidden,
quiet with hurricane
that had picked it up
on its way to
bigger fish.
she waits a few days in
emptiness of not weeping,
then carries her broom to where she had
huddled, her fraught breath her only
companion.

little left but the
loneliness
of discards,
she sweeps a small scribbled note
into the debris.
absentmindedly
pulls it from the floor pile
to her pocket,
where it stays forgotten as she
howls with such sorrow that
even the broom
shakes.
morning then and she
empties her pocket to find the
weathered paper.

> *the thief left it behind:*
> *the moon.*
> *at my window*
>   Ryokan
> 15th-century Japanese poet

she scorns its foolishness,
but still,
returns it to her pocket,
stroking it as she
trudges miles to
village shelter,
sleeping with haunted dreams of
displaced earth.

pulled by her beloved wind and
water and sand
she returns night after night
to the bones
of her house,
sitting by broken window frames,
sitting stillness of loss
moon now
luminous.

EARLY JUNE PEAS
Elizabeth Wallace

Large flatbed truck
speeding past our house on
Main Street,
pulling its bundled cargo of
Early June Peas to
our town cannery.
A few
blocks away is the
four corners stoplight,
where the trucks'
brief holding pattern
is our Mecca.

My brother and I have discovered
this delicacy in an earlier spillage.
> light green pods
> delicate and crunchy vines
> wound around each other as in
> Magical Forest.
> they are our apple in the
> Garden of Eden.

Soon they will be slaughtered,
sentenced to life in the can,
served at our table as forced consumption.
Crouching behind the early summer bushes,
waiting for the truck to stop,
we debate the church's position on stealing
and come up shorthanded.
Visions of a dark and suffocating
confessional loom large.
Our God is a punitive God.

In the moment of waiting and arrival
our bodies win and
with stealth and eagerness
we leap behind the truck
near wheels ready to roll
and in terror
both worldly and holy
we take and eat.

Prompt #4

THE UNKNOWING   Elizabeth Wallace

First light in nursery,
watercolors circle ceiling canvas,
sunbeams tickling thru slated crib,
green branches from white window
bringing dappled leaves into his
chubby hands. Moving his fingers every
which way in chase,
he shrieks
morning joy,
grabbing his toes
gulping his breath between peals
of laughter.
The day empties into him.

Night spreads and the old man
moves down from the still house,
carrying the frayed blanket
with great weariness and care,
placing the piece on grassy field.
Shivering with breeze,
moving in slow motion,
he lays to see stars,
his back cradling on yielding earth,
brittle bone, slack muscle, searching
for comfort.
Yes, all this he knows.

These nights he leaves the familiar bed
for what he cannot name. His breath not as
frail as they think,
his mind waiting for what he knows not.
He yields to strangeness,
to sounds of
rustling in the beyond,
to the movement of belly on dirt,
to the echo of hollow loneliness.
The dark wraps him and as the hours close
he stirs.
Wiping tears of wonder from his sunken cheeks,
he feels himself rise toward what he can finally
         love
this vast unfathomable mystery.

Prompt #30

FIREFLY FUGUE　　　　　　　　　Elizabeth Wallace

Evenings now, lingering sun,
giving sounds that whisper,
nudging our lazy attention.
Air breathing and humid, we wander to
porches, to lawns,
to flowering trees,
gazing at children
holding Mason jars
    as if
      chalices.

Waiting in hushed reverence,
we gasp at first sighting,
our chests swelling with joy at
swarming of shy twinkling
fireflies
released from far celestial
realms.

      come
        o
      come

circle us with radiance
as we sing as one
the old gospel hymn
"Shall We Gather at the River."

Prompt #17

WB Wieber

CHERRIES AND CHANCE

THE LONELY WIFE'S SECRET

WILD DOGWOOD

THE SONG OF EVERYWHEN

CHERRIES AND CHANCE — WB Wieber

Raven is hungry.
It's eyeing the young tree
whose sweet cherries
have been picked near clean.
What are the odds
that shiny bundle of coal-feathers,
harbinger of death, can tweak off
the last cherry dangling low under that tree?
It has to hop up from beneath, not fly,
make an awkward arrow of its beak
shoot for the prize.

Scientists say that it rains rubies
on Jupiter. They say particles
can sway each other instantaneously
from across the cosmos.
Is such celestial seduction what we call
Chance? Is it a heavenly swoon?
They say a particle can be and not-be
at the same time, unbound and
impossible, it could be several places at
once. Words and numbers
can't predict its popping in and out;
this is a total tease for physicists,
they have to look beyond the tangible,
open the gates to the soul.

A particle tangling with another particle
is sexy. That glimmering speck,
curious, charges towards another pulsing
smidgeon until they fuse and ignite.
Is that *Fate*? Microbes doze, atoms spark,
far Jupiter answers a warbling call;
with divinity's slingshot it
flings one ruby through a heart-
shaped hole in a soft fold of space.

On earth, what is the probability
that Death, unnoticed, will walk
past us tomorrow? Death
looks like every other stranger,
until one day you get that feathery feeling
you recognize someone and nod,
just once.
What a fateful cast:
hungry Raven, cherry tree plucked of
abundance, Jupiter enthralled,
Death (always a big player
whether or not it catches
your eye) invisible particles
charming each other
making time and space quiver,
and of course, there is always
You, beloved, on the other side
of every poem, our promise
that we will reach for each other
across any dark distance.

The finale:
famished for that last cherry,
though it had already lost out on
a whole tree's succulent crown,
elegant Raven swaggers off—
in its black beak, one red ruby.
And here, home again, your hand,
warm, still holding mine.

THE LONELY WIFE'S SECRET   WB Wieber

Just when she began
to feel home—her hands
wrist-deep in loam,
goldfinches stealing her seeds
(having tamed her)
a hummingbird, or swarm
of bees sufficient
to delight her steady
mated heart—
a neighbor spoke to her.
He was vivid in ways
she had not noticed.

As they leaned to talk,
he found a penny
on the ground between them.
He took her hand
in both of his, pressed
the coin into her palm
closed her fingers around it. It was
as if he thrust a whisper
into her heart, and her heart
held it.

Certain this would never
happen to her, she keeps
such foolishness hidden;
A small coin in her pocket,
compact, so very warm,
that she will not spend.

Prompt #31

WILD DOGWOOD   WB Wieber

At the church food pantry
she heard a man say, *ramps are up.*
Good thing, she thought,
all we got is pickles,
peanut butter and grits.

Home, she heads out into the damp wood
hunting fiddleheads, ramps,
morels. The boy stays in the bed,
coughing. She reaches into an opening
where spring sun warms the ground,
thinks, *it smells like perfume.*

She can still see far into the woods.
Even those last stubborn leaves
hanging on the beech, thin as cheesecloth,
were torn off in that big storm.
Hard winds combed moss-covered
twigs out of the trees, threw them down,
like Boy's dark hair
under the barber's chair.

Deep in the woods
before trees break bud
only the dogwood flowers.
She thinks to herself, *the white part,*
pretty, isn't a flower at all—
a cross of white petals
hugs the tiny green flowers
at the heart.

She carries home pungent
green bunches that smell of cold dirt
garlic and wild onion, heavy
as Mamaw's voice;
they'll cure what ails you,
Girl, but take less than half
so they come back each spring.
She picked them all
for Boy, had to.

Dogwood blooms low
against rough brown trunks,
pine needles and sharp un-sprung
leaf buds. In the shadows
one dogwood stands
alone, bright,
as if someone flung
a handful of moths up,
satin-white, into the dark air
and they hung there;
not rising, not falling,
quiet as hope.

> *If you have come here to help me, you are wasting your time.*
> *But if you have come because your liberation is bound up with*
> *mine, then let us work together.*
>   —Lilia Watson (A First Nation's Person living in Australia and a
>   Murri visual artist)

THE SONG OF EVERYWHEN   WB Wieber

She takes care of her Mother's
Mother's Country.
Her art is sacred.
From beneath the earth
her eyes burn holes upward,
through the sand and spear-grass
to where half-formed humans clash
until they fall out of life
in a cascade of disharmony—
red bones to red dust.

She takes us past the Black Stump,
Back of Beyond, the Never-Never
where sand plains and salt pans,
immobile, listen for their names.
Under hummocks of spikey grasses
termite grubs hunger, dragon lizards
dream, everlastings and cornflower
seeds hold their breath until rain;
maps of sacred hashmarks
and star-dots reveal
all paths connect.

She reminds us, *together*
we can sing back the unspoiled.
From this desolate landscape
between now and tomorrow, *together*
we can sing free
our unbroken beings,
awaken the names of every river,
rock and root, every creature,
winged or tailed, and *together*
heal the heart's land,
until it ripples with wildflowers
and welcomes us home.

Prompt #24

Notes on Contributors

Victoria Bender notes that had she been braver we would have heard of her already—if she had been more driven, more ambitious. Writing poetry may have been her untold want, but somehow has become a need. She is sending out her poems over the internet, in print, in person. If you like it, pass it on. This is insurgent art.

Carol Booth tells us that, after careers in teaching mathematics, parenting, and (mostly) bankruptcy law, she looked for different challenges in retirement. A series of poetry classes at OLLI provided just the challenge she needed and led to a new passion and a wonderful community.

Karen Depew has lived in Asheville since 2013. She grew up in Philadelphia, but has lived in the San Francisco Bay area, Boston, and Washington, DC. For twenty years she had an Executive Coaching company. She has been published in *Smoky Blue Literary & Arts Magazine* and *Steam Ticket*.

Kay Duncan is a former editor and art director who made Houston her home. Since retiring and moving to Asheville seven years ago, she has plunged wholeheartedly into OLLI, with a double major in art and poetry. Like Zonker Harris of *Doonesbury*, she steers clear of graduating.

Kim Hayes spent her early years fishing with her dad, going to Sunday school, swimming, reading, and playing piano. She has applied her English degree to writing positions in radio, finance, and hospitality, never abandoning her first love—poetry. Kim has treasured the encouragement and inspiration of the poetry community at OLLI.

Richard Horvath was born in Bridgeport, Connecticut in 1942. He graduated from Oberlin College and was drafted in 1964. Richard moved to lower east side Manhattan 1966 where he acquired an enduring New York state of mind. He moved to Asheville in 2009 with wife Sylvie and began writing poems. Richard likes music, chess, baseball, and good seafood.

Notes on Contributors

Jay Jacoby, a now-retired English professor, has lived in North Carolina for the past 42 years, the last 20 in Asheville. His poetry has appeared in a number of journals including the *Asheville Poetry Review, Frisson, Cold Mountain Review,* and the *Main Street Rag*. Jay has offered classes at OLLI since 2002.

Ann Tobias Karson grew up in South Africa, becoming an anti-apartheid activist in her twenties. Interspersed with a career in Clinical Social Work in Psychiatry and living in three countries (South Africa, England, and the US), Ann would write the occasional verse. She took an OLLI poetry class in 1995. Her poems have since been published in several journals.

Bill Petz had careers in ministry, higher education, public health, and criminal justice. He has used poetry as a bridge to awareness and understanding with folks with chronic illness, health care providers, men's groups, and OLLI members. He and his wife are long-time residents of the Asheville area.

Nelson Sartoris was a professor at Wittenberg University in Ohio, where he chaired the Chemistry Department. On a whim five years ago, he took a course on writing poetry. Since then, he has published three collections, *Brain Slivers, On Wings of Words,* and *With These Hands*.

Sarah Scott was a television news producer, a corporate and independent video writer/producer/director, and a TV/video manager for the state of Washington's House of Representatives. Following an off-grid life on Mt. Rainier's haunches, this east Tennessee native moved to Asheville in mid-2019. Her published mystery is *Lies at Six*.

Judith Farley Upjohn returned to poetry after a career in alternative education. Her chapbooks and book-objects include *Alice in Ribbons, You can't get milk from an earlobe: primal time at the (cafe wha?), Glamour & the Clam,* and *Too Long in the Reliquary*. Recent readings or publications include Malaprops Books, *Great Smokies Review,* and *Word of Mouth* online.

ELIZABETH WALLACE notes that her profession as a speech language therapist and her experiences as a reader with Irish roots led her to embrace poetry in easy and difficult times. Years of classes and OLLI groups have helped bring her poetry to paper and to her textile artwork. What a wonderful way to live.

WENDY B. WIEBER began writing poetry again after a long hiatus, thanks to OLLI and the Barricaded Bards. She grew up in the Northeast, lived for many years in California, and returned East in 1991. She retired from a career as a special educator several years ago. Wendy and her wife Elizabeth moved to Fairview 12 years ago.

Also available from Pisgah Press & ArsPoetica

Letting Go: Collected Poems 1983-2003 — Donna Lisle Burton (1929-2020)
$14.95 (AP)
Way Past Time for Reflecting
$17.95 (AP)
From Roots ... to Wings
$17.95 (AP)

This Virgin Page — Jim Carillon
$12.00 (AP)

Gabriel's Songbook — Michael A. Cody
$17.95
A Twilight Reel
$17/95

Musical Morphine: Transforming Pain One Note at a Time — Robin Russell Gaiser
$17.95 Finalist, USA Book Awards for Health: Alternative Medicine, 2017
Open for Lunch
$17.95

A Freethinker's Gospel: Essays for a Sacred Secular World — Chris Highland
$17.95

...and to see takes time — Mamie Hilliard
$12.00 (AP)

The Last of the Swindlers — Peter Loewer
$17.95

Swords in their Hands: George Washington and the Newburgh Conspiracy
$24.95 Finalist, USA Book Awards for History, 2014 Dave Richards

Reed's Homophones: A Comprehensive Book of Sound-alike Words — A. D. Reed
$14.95

Brain Slivers — Nelson Sartoris
$12.99 (AP)
On Wings of Words
$12.00 (AP)
With These Hands
$15.00 (AP)

Trang Sen: A Novel of Vietnam — Sarah-Ann Smith
$19.50

Invasive Procedures: Earthqukes, Calamities, & poems from the midst of life — Nan Socolow
$17.95 (AP)

Deadly Dancing   THE RICK RYDER MYSTERY SERIES   RF Wilson
$15.95
Killer Weed
$14.95
The Pot Professor
$15.95

To order:

Pisgah Press, LLC
PO Box 9663, Asheville, NC 28815-0663
www.pisgahpress.com

www.ingramcontent.com/pod-product-compliance
Lightning Source LLC
Chambersburg PA
CBHW071712040426
42446CB00011B/2026